Changeover Observation Form

Department:_____   Process: _____   Date:_____

Step	Task / Operation	Task Time in Seconds		Observation / Improvement Idea / Comment
		External	Internal	
	Subtotal for Each			

Internal: Only can be done when the machine is stopped.
External: Can be done while the machine is running.

www.enna.com
www.productivitypress.com

Changeover Observation Form

Department:_____ Process: _____ Date:_____

Step	Task / Operation	Task Time in Seconds		Observation / Improvement Idea / Comment
		External	Internal	
Subtotal for Each				**Internal:** Only can be done when the machine is stopped.
				External: Can be done while the machine is running.

www.enna.com
www.productivitypress.com

Changeover Observation Form

Department:_____ Process:_____ Date:_____

Step	Task / Operation	Task Time in Seconds		Observation / Improvement Idea / Comment
		External	Internal	
	Subtotal for Each			**Internal:** Only can be done when the machine is stopped. **External:** Can be done while the machine is running.

www.enna.com
www.productivitypress.com

Changeover Observation Form

Department:_____ Process:_____ Date:_____

Step	Task / Operation	Task Time in Seconds		Observation / Improvement Idea / Comment
		External	**Internal**	
	Subtotal for Each			**Internal:** Only can be done when the machine is stopped. **External:** Can be done while the machine is running.

www.enna.com
www.productivitypress.com

Changeover Observation Form

Department:_____   Process:_____   Date:_____

Step	Task / Operation	Task Time in Seconds		Observation / Improvement Idea / Comment
		External	Internal	
	Subtotal for Each			

Internal: Only can be done when the machine is stopped.
External: Can be done while the machine is running.

www.enna.com
www.productivitypress.com

Changeover Observation Form

Department:_____   Process:_____   Date:_____

Step	Task / Operation	Task Time in Seconds		Observation / Improvement Idea / Comment
		External	Internal	
	Subtotal for Each			

Internal: Only can be done when the machine is stopped.
External: Can be done while the machine is running.

Changeover Observation Form

Department:_____ Process:_____ Date:_____

Step	Task / Operation	Task Time in Seconds		Observation / Improvement Idea / Comment
		External	**Internal**	
	Subtotal for Each			

Internal: Only can be done when the machine is stopped.
External: Can be done while the machine is running.

www.enna.com
www.productivitypress.com

Changeover Observation Form

Department:_____   Process:_____   Date:_____

Step	Task / Operation	Task Time in Seconds		Observation / Improvement Idea / Comment
		External	Internal	
	Subtotal for Each			**Internal:** Only can be done when the machine is stopped. **External:** Can be done while the machine is running.

Changeover Observation Form

Department:_____ Process:_____ Date:_____

Step	Task / Operation	Task Time in Seconds		Observation / Improvement Idea / Comment
		External	Internal	
Subtotal for Each				

Internal: Only can be done when the machine is stopped.
External: Can be done while the machine is running.

Changeover Observation Form

Department:_____   Process:_____   Date:_____

Step	Task / Operation	Task Time in Seconds		Observation / Improvement Idea / Comment
		External	Internal	
	Subtotal for Each			

Internal: Only can be done when the machine is stopped.
External: Can be done while the machine is running.

www.enna.com
www.productivitypress.com

Changeover Observation Form

Department:_____   Process:_____   Date:_____

Step	Task / Operation	Task Time in Seconds		Observation / Improvement Idea / Comment
		External	**Internal**	
	Subtotal for Each			**Internal:** Only can be done when the machine is stopped. **External:** Can be done while the machine is running.

www.enna.com
www.productivitypress.com

Changeover Observation Form

Department:_____   Process:_____   Date:_____

Step	Task / Operation	Task Time in Seconds		Observation / Improvement Idea / Comment
		External	Internal	
Subtotal for Each				

Internal: Only can be done when the machine is stopped.
External: Can be done while the machine is running.

Changeover Observation Form

Department:_____   Process:_____   Date:_____

Step	Task / Operation	Task Time in Seconds		Observation / Improvement Idea / Comment
		External	**Internal**	
	Subtotal for Each			

Internal: Only can be done when the machine is stopped.
External: Can be done while the machine is running.

Changeover Observation Form

Department:_____ Process:_____ Date:_____

Step	Task / Operation	Task Time in Seconds		Observation / Improvement Idea / Comment
		External	Internal	
	Subtotal for Each			**Internal:** Only can be done when the machine is stopped. **External:** Can be done while the machine is running.

www.enna.com
www.productivitypress.com

Changeover Observation Form

Department:_____ Process:_____ Date:_____

Step	Task / Operation	Task Time in Seconds		Observation / Improvement Idea / Comment
		External	Internal	
	Subtotal for Each			**Internal:** Only can be done when the machine is stopped. **External:** Can be done while the machine is running.

www.enna.com
www.productivitypress.com

Changeover Observation Form

Department:_____ Process: _____ Date:_____

Step	Task / Operation	Task Time in Seconds		Observation / Improvement Idea / Comment
		External	Internal	
	Subtotal for Each			**Internal:** Only can be done when the machine is stopped. **External:** Can be done while the machine is running.

Changeover Observation Form

Department:_____   Process:_____   Date:_____

Step	Task / Operation	Task Time in Seconds		Observation / Improvement Idea / Comment
		External	**Internal**	
	Subtotal for Each			

Internal: Only can be done when the machine is stopped.
External: Can be done while the machine is running.

www.enna.com
www.productivitypress.com

Changeover Observation Form

Department:_____ Process:_____ Date:_____

Step	Task / Operation	Task Time in Seconds		Observation / Improvement Idea / Comment
		External	Internal	
	Subtotal for Each			**Internal:** Only can be done when the machine is stopped.
				External: Can be done while the machine is running.

www.enna.com
www.productivitypress.com

Changeover Observation Form

Department:_____   Process:_____   Date:_____

Step	Task / Operation	Task Time in Seconds		Observation / Improvement Idea / Comment
		External	Internal	
	Subtotal for Each			

Internal: Only can be done when the machine is stopped.
External: Can be done while the machine is running.

www.enna.com
www.productivitypress.com

Changeover Observation Form

Department:_____ Process:_____ Date:_____

Step	Task / Operation	Task Time in Seconds		Observation / Improvement Idea / Comment
		External	Internal	
Subtotal for Each				

Internal: Only can be done when the machine is stopped.
External: Can be done while the machine is running.

www.enna.com
www.productivitypress.com

Changeover Observation Form

Department:_____   Process: _____   Date:_____

Step	Task / Operation	Task Time in Seconds		Observation / Improvement Idea / Comment
		External	Internal	
Subtotal for Each				

Internal: Only can be done when the machine is stopped.
External: Can be done while the machine is running.

www.enna.com
www.productivitypress.com

Changeover Observation Form

Department:_____ Process:_____ Date:_____

Step	Task / Operation	Task Time in Seconds		Observation / Improvement Idea / Comment
		External	**Internal**	
	Subtotal for Each			**Internal:** Only can be done when the machine is stopped. **External:** Can be done while the machine is running.

Changeover Observation Form

Department:_____ Process:_____ Date:_____

Step	Task / Operation	Task Time in Seconds		Observation / Improvement Idea / Comment
		External	**Internal**	
Subtotal for Each				

Internal: Only can be done when the machine is stopped.
External: Can be done while the machine is running.

Changeover Observation Form

Department:_____ Process: _____ Date:_____

Step	Task / Operation	Task Time in Seconds		Observation / Improvement Idea / Comment
		External	Internal	
	Subtotal for Each			

Internal: Only can be done when the machine is stopped.
External: Can be done while the machine is running.

www.enna.com
www.productivitypress.com

Changeover Observation Form

Department:_____ Process:_____ Date:_____

Step	Task / Operation	Task Time in Seconds		Observation / Improvement Idea / Comment
		External	Internal	
Subtotal for Each				

Internal: Only can be done when the machine is stopped.
External: Can be done while the machine is running.